THE BASICS OF

WINNING BRIDGE

Montgomery Coe

- Gambling Research Institute -
Cardoza Publishing

Cardoza Publishing is the foremost gaming publisher in the world with a library of more than 175 up-to-date and easy-to-read books and strategies. These authoritative works are written by the top experts in their fields and with more than 8,500,000 books in print, represent the best-selling and most popular gaming books anywhere.

FOURTH EDITION
Third Printing

Copyright © 1989, 1993, 1999, 2002 by Cardoza Publishing
- All Rights Reserved -

ISBN: 1-58042-055-9
Library of Congress Catalog No: 2002101325

Visit our website—www.cardozapub.com—or write for a full list of Cardoza books and advanced strategies.

CARDOZA PUBLISHING

P.O. Box 1500, Cooper Station, New York, NY 10276
Phone (800)577-WINS
email: cardozapub@aol.com
www.cardozapub.com

Table of Contents

Charts

I. Introduction

Bridge is one of the most popular games ever invented by man, and has been around since 1926, during which time it has attracted millions of players. The game is basically a partnership game combining a great deal of skill with a little luck, and in some forms, such as duplicate where teams of four play, it is a game of pure skill.

The game of bridge has two distinct parts; the bidding and the play of the hand, and in this book, we're going to go step by step, to show you how the game is played, bid, scored, and all other information necessary for you to start playing with a partner.

Once you learn the game of rubber bridge, the standard game played in people's homes, and the one we'll discuss, you'll find it fascinating. And the game, unlike games like gin rummy and poker, can be played without stakes or money. The skill in itself is pleasure enough.

Let's now look at the game, from the beginning, and go step by step through all the information that you'll need to make yourself a competent bridge player.

II. The Basics of Bridge

The Cards

The game is played with a pack of 52 cards, without the jokers, which are discarded. The ordinary pack of cards is often called a bridge deck. It consists of four distinct suits, two red and two black. In bridge, unlike many other games, the suits have distinct values. The best and highest suit is spades, followed by hearts, diamonds and clubs.

Each suit contains thirteen cards, ranging from the ace, which is the highest, down to the 2, which is the lowest. The ranking of cards is as follows from highest to lowest: ace, king, queen, jack, 10, 9, 8, 7, 6, 5, 4, 3 and finally the 2. For purposes of this book, we will use the following abbreviations: ace = A, king = K, queen = Q and jack = J. All the other cards will be called by their numerical connotation, i.e., the 8 = 8.

We have named the order of the suits, from the spade suit down to the clubs. Spades and hearts, the two highest ranking suits, are known as the **major suits.** The other two, diamonds and clubs, are known as **minor suits.** As we shall see, there will be a difference in the suits, both in bidding and scoring.

When we state that the ace is the highest ranking of the cards in any suit, it means that, in the course of play, an ace will win any individual round of play in which all four cards played out will be of the same suit. For example, if all hearts are played as follows: jack, 9, king and ace; the ace will win the trick being the highest.

But before we go into the playing out of hands, let's examine the procedures necessary to begin a game of contract bridge.

The Partnership

We're going to discuss the private game of bridge, which is known as **rubber bridge.** In this game, two partnerships play against each other, and the goal of each partnership is to win two games before the other partnership does. Two games then constitutes a **rubber.** Once a team has won a rubber, then new games are played to see who wins the next rubber.

Before the game begins, the partnerships may be chosen by the drawing of cards, with the two highest cards constituting one partnership, or prior to play, two individuals may decide to become partners, without random choosing by drawing of cards. In any event, one team will be known as the **North-South** pair, and the other as the **East-West** pair.

Here's how it will look at the table:

N

W   **E**

S

Bidding and play is always in a clockwise fashion, so later on in the book, we may describe the bidding in the following sequence, for example:

North   **East**   **South**   **West**

But for now, let's assume that the partnerships have been formed, one being North-South, and the other East-West. The players will stay in the same seats and play in the same sequence until a rubber is complete, at which time they may either form new partnerships, or change places at the table, so that the North-South pair will now become the East-West pair.

Shuffling and Dealing

Two decks of cards should be used for rubber bridge. One deck will be in play, while the other will have been shuffled and be ready to be dealt. The best way to do this is to have two different and distinct colored backs on the cards, such as one deck being red and the other blue, so that the cards won't be mixed up.

The cards in one deck are cut to see who gets the highest card. The highest card becomes the dealer. He shuffles up the cards and then gives them to the player on his right to be cut, then the cards are restacked and then dealt out. Let's assume that the North player has had high card and is the dealer. He shuffles up one deck, while his partner shuffles up the other deck. Once the second deck has been fully shuffled by South, he puts them to his right, so that, in the next deal, East will take those cards from the second deck, give them to the North player to cut, then East will deal them out. While East does this in the second round of play, his partner, West, will be shuffling up the first deck, which was previously played out.

Now that North has restacked the deck after West cut it, he proceeds to deal out the cards one at a time, till all 52 cards are completely dealt out. The deal is clockwise, so East will get the first card, then South, then West and finally North. When the cards are fully dealt out, then each player will have thirteen cards in his or her hand, ready for the first part of bridge, the bidding. So, in the next section, we'll deal with the fundamentals of bidding. But before we do this, we should now study the object of the game, to see the purpose of bidding.

Object of the Game

The object of bridge is to bid for a particular contract and then win enough rounds of cards, known as **tricks**, to justify that bid. If partnership bids and makes as many or more tricks than the bid called for, the partnership will be rewarded with points. If it fails to make the tricks needed to justify the bid, it is said to **go down**, or **be set** and the other side is rewarded with points.

In bridge, the first six tricks are considered as a base and are never bid. These six tricks are known as **book**. The bidding will start at the one-level. If a partnership bids one in a particular suit, for example, it means it has to make seven tricks to win; the six base tricks, and the one bid. If the bid is two, it has to make eight tricks. If the bid is seven, the highest, it has to win all the tricks to justify its contract.

So, the object of the game is to bid correctly, so that the partnership that is awarded the final bid, makes enough tricks to get points. On the other hand, the other team, the defenders of the contract, want to play expertly enough to defeat the contract, making enough tricks on their part to **set the contract**, to get points on their side.

III. Fundamentals of Bidding

There are any number of bids possible by each player. If he or she has a very weak hand, and can't make sufficient tricks, he or she can **pass.** The pass, therefore, is the weakest of all bids. However, a player can pass, and then re-enter the contract later on with a different bid. Passing doesn't foreclose anything.

Then the next bids can be in a suit. At the one-level, it would be One Heart or One Spade or One Club or One Diamond, depending on the strength of the individual hand. The purpose of reaching a final bid in a particular suit is to make that suit **trumps** so that it has precedence over other suits.

Trumps becomes important in the playing out of the hand, because when a player is out of a particular suit, he may play a trump from his hand and win the round or trick, even though his trump is the lowest ranking card on the table.

For example, hearts are trump. An ace of spades has been played, then a king of spades, then a queen of spades, and the fourth player who is out of spades, plays the 2 of hearts and wins the trick, because a trump is always higher than any led suit. But in this situation, one can only play a trump if he or she is out of the led suit. If that same player, the fourth one, had another spade in his hand, he'd have to play it.

Let's follow a sample bidding round and see what it entails. We'll assume that North was the dealer and thus the first bidder.

North	East	South	West
1 Club	Pass	2 Clubs	Pass
Pass	Pass		

North's One Club bid was an **opening bid.** Or, it might be stated that North *opened One Club.* South *responded* with Two Clubs. Once a bid has been made, and there are three consecutive passes following it, as in the above diagram, the bidding ends. Thus, the above contract is for Two Clubs.

This means that North and South must make at least eight tricks $(6 + 2)$ in order to make the contract. East and West need six tricks to set it. Since clubs is trump, and since North first bid clubs, North will play out the hands of both North and South. South will become the **dummy.** North is said to be the **declarer.** East and West are the **defenders.**

Now, we must remember the order of the suits. Spades is the highest, followed by Hearts, then Diamonds and then Clubs. Let's say the bidding had gone as follows:

North	East	South	West
1 Club	Pass	1 Spade	Pass

At this point, if North wanted to make another bid, he could either bid One No-Trump or have to go into the two level for his next bid. A **No-Trump** bid means just what it implies; the hand is played with no particular suit as trump. If the final contract is in No-Trump, then all suits have equal value, and the highest ranked card of any suit led will win the trick.

Let's continue the bidding of the previous hand.

North	East	South	West
1 Club	Pass	1 Spade	Pass
1 No-Trump	Pass	2 Spades	Pass
3 Clubs	Pass	5 Clubs	Pass
Pass	Pass		

After North bid 1 No-Trump, South had to bid into the two-level, and then North, in responding again, had to either bid 2 No-Trump (the only bid remaining in the two-level), or go to the three level, which he did with a bid of Three Clubs. Note then that South jumped to Five Clubs. The bidding doesn't have to go up one at a time, it can jump anytime. Let's see the next example, where all sides get into the bidding.

North	East	South	West
1 Heart	2 Diamonds	2 Hearts	2 Spades
3 Hearts	4 Spades	Pass	Pass
Pass			

After some spirited bidding on both sides, in which East jumped his partners bid from 2 to 4 Spades, the contract was awarded to the East-West pair at 4 Spades.

Since West first bid Spades, the trump suit, he gets to play out the hand, while East will become the dummy. The North-South pair will defend. East-West needs 10 tricks (6 + 4) to make the contract while the other pair needs only four tricks to set it.

Let's review what we know about bidding so far:

1. The dealer is the first one to bid. He may make any bid, including Pass.

2. The bidding then goes in clockwise order around the table. Everyone can bid; even someone who passed the first time around.

3. The lowest suit bid is clubs, followed by diamonds, then hearts, spades and no-trump. After a bid in a lower level, if the next bid is a suit that is lower than the previously bid suit, the bid must be at a higher level. Thus, after a bid of Two Hearts, a bid in Diamonds would have to be at least Three Diamonds.

4. After a bid of a suit or no-trump, three consecutive passes end the bidding.

5. The highest bidder as a pair plays for the contract. The other pair defends.

6. When a bid is complete, the pair getting the contract must make the bid number plus six additional tricks to win. For example, if the bid is Three Hearts, the declarer must make nine tricks altogether, the three bid plus six other tricks (base tricks).

7. The goal of the defenders is to set the contract by making enough tricks so that the declarer doesn't make his contract. Since there are 13 tricks altogether, one for each card dealt to each player, if the bid is four, then the defenders must make four tricks to defeat the contract. If they make their four, the declarer can only make nine tricks, and needed ten because of his bid.

Note that two of the final bids were Five Clubs and Four Spades. There is a reason for these final bids. To win a game, a partnership must make at least 100 points as a result of bidding and playing out a hand or hands. Here's how the scoring goes:

IV. Scoring

Before we give the scores for each situation, we will show you what a score sheet looks like.

We   **They**

Note the horizontal line separating each section. Scoring is done both below and above that line. Below the line are the trick or game scores, while above it are the overtricks, undertricks, doubling, redoubling and previous game scores.

The Game Score

Now let's discuss the **game score**. The goal is to get 100 points below the line to win a game. Here's how this is done:

The minor suits, Clubs and Diamonds, each have a value of 20 points for each bid above **book**. By book we mean the six tricks figured as base tricks.

If the final bid by a partnership had been Two Clubs, then the total points made by the partnership, if they make the contract, is 40 points, or 2 x 20 points. If the bid had been Five Clubs, then it would be 100 points, or 5 x 20 points.

Thus we now know that the minor suits are counted at 20 points per bid.

The major suits, Spades and Hearts, on the other hand, have a value of 30 points bid above book. Thus, a Three Spade bid made would yield 90 points, or 3 x 30 points. That's not enough for a game. A bid of Four in a major suit, or Five in a minor suit, is sufficient for game by itself, if the contract is made. That's why we saw the Four Spade bid before.

No-Trump counts as 40 points for the first one bid, and 30 points thereafter. Thus, a bid of Two No-Trump made by the declarer would yield 70 points, and Three No-Trump would yield game of 100 points.

Let's recapitulate what we know about scoring so far:

```
┌─────────────────────────────────────────────┐
│                   Chart 1                    │
│          Suit and No-Trump Scoring           │
│                                              │
│  Suit                 Value of Each Trick Bid│
│  Spades               30 points              │
│  Hearts               30 points              │
│  Diamonds             20 points              │
│  Clubs                20 points              │
│  No-Trump             40 points - first trick│
│  No-Trump             30 points - thereafter │
└─────────────────────────────────────────────┘
```

Now, you might ask, what happens if the bid is Two Spades and the declarer makes three, or **one overtrick.** He would get credit for 60 points below the line, and an additional 30 points above the line. To get the full 90 points below the line, where it is more valuable, the declarer's final bid would have to be Three Spades. Here's how the overtrick scoring would look:

We		They
30		
60		

Before we go any further, let's now discuss another aspect of the game that affects both bidding and scoring.

Doubles and Redoubles

So far, we've seen bids of either a suit, no-trump or pass. But there's another bid that can be made, and that is a **Double**. And then there's a **Redouble** as well. Doubles can be used as other than penalty bids, but right now, we'll discuss them as purely penalty bids. A player makes a doubling bid if he or she thinks that the contract can't be made by the other team, and wants to score penalty points. Here's what a bidding sequence might look like:

North	East	South	West
1 Heart	1 Spade	2 Hearts	2 Spades
4 Hearts	Pass	Pass	Double
Pass	Pass	Pass	

West's Double signifies that he doesn't believe that North, as declarer, can make ten tricks. After West's double, everyone else can bid, either a suit or no-trump or a redouble. Since no one did this, the final contract is at Four Hearts, doubled. If North playing out the hand, makes his Four Hearts, he'll get extra bonus points for doing this; in fact his *below-the-line* score would be doubled. If he failed to make Four Hearts, then the other team woudl get a bonus score above-the-line on their side.

First, let's show a situation where the contract is Doubled and then Redoubled. We'll go back to the previous rounds of bidding.

North	East	South	West
1 Heart	1 Spade	2 Hearts	2 Spades
4 Hearts	Pass	Pass	Double
Redouble	Pass	Pass	Pass

North has redoubled, which means that he thinks he can make his contract, and he's fishing for even more points. If he makes his contract, he gets all these points below the line. If he is set, the points go to the other side above the line.

Vulnerable and Not Vulnerable

We must also explain these terms in scoring. Since in rubber bridge, a partnership must win two games to win the rubber, the team ahead by one game is penalized in the scoring by being considered **vulnerable.** Suppose this is the score at the end of the first game:

We	They
100	60

The "We" team had bid and made Three No-Trump after the "They" team had bid and made Two Spades. By scoring 100 points below the line, the "We" team has won the first game, and is now vulnerable. Scoring for the second game would thus begin like this, with the 100 points placed above the line, carried over from the first game on behalf of the "We" team, and 60 points on behalf of the "They" team.

We	They
100	60

In the second game, the "We" team is vulnerable and the "They" team is not-vulnerable. If the "They" team won the second game, *both* teams would now be vulnerable. Having understood this concept, let's show all the scoring, including doubled and redoubled hands, vulnerable and not vulnerable.

Chart 2
Double and Redoubled Scoring

Suit	Value of Each Trick Bid	Value of Each Doubled Trick	Value of Each Redoubled Trick
Spades	30	60	120
Hearts	30	60	120
Diamonds	20	40	80
Clubs	20	40	80
No-Trump (First Trick)	40	80	160
No-Trump Each Additional Trick)	30	60	120

If a bid is doubled and made or redoubled and made, *that score goes below the line.* Thus, a bid of Two Spades, which is only worth 60 points, if doubled and made, is now worth 120 points, and is scored below the line. Even though Two Spades wouldn't be sufficient to win a game, since it's doubled to 120 points, it now wins the game. This is called **doubling into game.**

Now, let's look at above-the-line scores. None of these affect the 100 points necessary to win a game, but are additional points used to add up the final score. Whichever partnership has the highest score after a complete rubber is played, has won.

Overtricks and Undertricks

We've mentioned these concepts in passing; now let's explain them more fully. An **overtrick** is an extra trick made by the declarer. For example, if he bid Five Diamonds and made twelve tricks, he made one overtrick, since he was obligated only to win eleven tricks to make his contract.

An **undertrick** is the opposite. If a declarer bid Five Diamonds, and only made ten tricks, he is set one trick, which is an undertrick. Both overtricks and undertricks *are scored above the line,* and don't count toward game score of 100.

Overtricks

These are tricks made above those bid for in the contract. If nine tricks are required to make the contract and ten tricks were actually made, there would be one overtrick.

Chart 3 Overtrick Scoring		
Each Overtrick	**Not Vulnerable**	**Vulnerable**
Undoubled	Ordinary Trick Value*	Ordinary Trick Value*
Doubled	100	200
Redoubled	200	400

* By ordinary trick value, we mean 30 points for each major suit (spades, hearts) and 20 points for each minor suit (diamonds, clubs).

Undertricks

Undertricks are deficiencies of tricks made after a bid. For example, if four spades is bid, meaning that ten tricks have to be won to make the contract, and only nine tricks were made, there's one undertrick. This score of course, goes to the defending team.

Chart 4
Undertrick Scoring: Undoubled Contract

Undoubled Contracts	Not Vulnerable	Vulnerable
First Undertrick	50	100
Each Additional Undertrick	50	100

Chart 5
Undertrick Scoring: Doubled Contract

Doubled Contracts	Not Vulnerable	Vulnerable
First Undertrick	100	200
2nd & 3rd Undertrick	200	300
Each Additional Undertrick	300	300

Chart 6
Undertrick Scoring: Redoubled Contracts

Rodoubled Contracts	Not Vulnerable	Vulnerable
First Undertrick	200	400
2nd & 3rd Undertrick	400	600
Each Additional Undertrick	600	600

Let's show some examples to make the scoring concept perfectly clear.

Example 1: The bid is Two Spades doubled. The declarer "We" is not vulnerable and makes one overtrick.

We	They
100	
120	

The contract is doubled into game as a result of the double, and since there was a double, the overtrick is worth 100 points instead of the ordinary 30 points.

Example 2: Both sides are vulnerable. The bid by "We" is Five Clubs, doubled. The declarer can only make three clubs, and thus there are two undertricks.

We	They
	500

As we can see by the previous table, a doubled contract that is vulnerable is penalized 200 points for the first undertrick and 300 points for each undertrick thereafter. Thus the penalty garnered by the "They" team is 500 points.

Remember, these penalty points are above-the-line and don't affect the 100 points needed for game.

Premium Points

All premium points which encompass slams and honor points are scored above the line.

Slams

Bidding and making twelve tricks, a bid of Six in any suit or six no-trump, is called a **small slam**. A bid of Seven in any suit or no-trump, made, is called a **grand slam**.

```
┌─────────────────────────────────────────────┐
│                  Chart 7                      │
│               Slam Scoring                    │
│                                               │
│              Not Vulnerable    Vulnerable     │
│ Small Slam        500             750         │
│ Grand Slam        1000            1500        │
│   Doubling or redoubling doesn't affect slam  │
│   points.                                     │
└─────────────────────────────────────────────┘
```

Honor Points

Additional points are awarded a team that has certain high cards, called honors. Honors are the A K Q J 10 of the trump suit.

```
┌─────────────────────────────────────────────┐
│                  Chart 8                      │
│               Honor Points                    │
│                                               │
│ Holding all five honors         150 points   │
│ Holding four out of five        100 points   │
│ Holding all four aces in a      150 points   │
│      No-Trump contract                        │
└─────────────────────────────────────────────┘
```

Vulnerability, doubling or redoubling doesn't affect honor points. (Note that the 10 is considered an *Honor* for scoring purposes only, and later, in our discussion of hands, when we speak of honors, we're referring only to the A, K, Q and J.)

Rubber Points

Additional points are given to the team winning the rubber, by winning both games. These are scored above the line.

Chart 9
Rubber Points

Winning Rubber	- two games to none	700 points
Winning Rubber	- two games to one	500 points
Unfinished Rubber	- winning one game	300 points
Unfinished Game	- part score	100 points

Doubling and redoubling doesn't affect rubber premium points.

There is one other premium point situation, and that is the making of any doubled or redoubled contract. An additional 50 points is awarded for making a doubled contract and 100 points for a redoubled contract whether the declaring team is vulnerable or not vulnerable. This is scored above the line by the declarer's side.

The Final Score

The final score is a total of all points made by each partnership below and above the line in a rubber. For example, if the "We" team scored 200 points below the line in winning two games, and an additional 1100 points above the line, it would have a total of 1300 points.

If the "They" team socred 120 points below the line and 600 above the line, it would have a total of 720 points. Therefore, the "We" team would win 1300 to 720, a margin of 580 points.

V. How To Play Out Hands

We've been discussing the winning of tricks throug-
out our discussion of bidding and points, and so, let's
digress and show just how a hand is played out after
the bidding. First, let's see the bidding.

North	East	South	West
1 Spade	2 Hearts	4 Spades	Pass
Pass	Pass		

In the bidding sequence above, South jumped his
bid to Four Spades, in order to shut out the other
team. Bids give information, as we shall see, and by
the jump bid, South foreclosed the other team from
bidding at a lower level to gain information. And Four
Spades is a game bid.

North becomes the declarer, since North first bid
the Spade suit, which is trumps. South becomes the
dummy. By dummy, we mean that South doesn't par-
ticipate in the playing out of the hand. *After the first
lead,* he simply puts down his cards. Declarer will play
out both hands in order.

The defenders, East and West, retain their cards in their hands, and play them out against the declarer. Thus, the defenders see one of the declarer's hands open, while their hands are not seen by the declarer.

After the bidding has ended the player to the right of the dummy makes the first lead. This is one of the defenders, not the declarer. This is an important concept in bridge - it is the defending team, not the declarer, that leads first.

Before we go any further, let's now look at all the cards being held by the two teams, prior to the first play.

North
♠ A Q J 3 2
♥ 7 6
♦ K J 10 9
♣ J 3

West
♠ 5
♥ Q J 8 3
♦ 6 2
♣ A 10 9 8 5 4

East
♠ K 6 4
♥ A K 10 9 5 4
♦ Q 8 3
♣ 2

South
♠ 10 9 8 7
♥ 2
♦ A 7 5 4
♣ K Q 7 6

The above diagram is how bridge games are shown, so that you can follow the progress of play in your daily newspaper, if you desire. North is the declarer, and

South becomes dummy. The first lead is by East, the player sitting to the right of the dummy.

Let's assume that East leads his singleton ♣ 2, hoping that West has the ace, so that West can not only take the trick, but return another club which East can now trump for another won trick.

Here's how the first round of play would look. East leads the ♣ 2, South (with North as declarer playing out the cards, since South is the dummy) the ♣ 6, West the ♣ A and North the ♣ 3. West has won the trick with the ace of clubs. He now leads. In contract bridge, the winner of the previous trick leads the next trick, another important concept to remember, for the winner of a trick has control of what to lead for the next round of play.

On this second round, West leads the 10 of clubs, North follows suit with the ♣ J, and now East, void in clubs, trumps with the ♠ 4, while South must put on the ♣ 7. Thus East wins the trick with his trump, and already East-West have won two tricks while North-South have won none. Since the contract is Four Spades, East-West must win two more tricks in order to set the contract.

After each won trick, the player winning the trick will put all four cards together forming a **packet** and place the packet in front of him or her. Thus it is easy to know how many tricks have been won by either side. The declarer places his won packets in front of him, for he is playing out both his and dummy's hands.

Remember, once a suit is led, it must be followed as long as a player has a card in that suit in his hand. We saw that in the first trick played. In the second trick, East was out of clubs, so he was able to play trump. He didn't have to play trumps if void in the led suit; he could have played any other suit. For example, if his partner, West, also had the king of clubs, and that would win the trick, East could have **sluffed off,** or gotten rid of a card from any other suit, if he desired.

In No-Trump contracts, there is no trumps to play, so if a player is void in the led suit, he cannot win that trick. His other suit played is useless as far as winning a trick is concerned. Suppose that this contract had been played in No-Trump. The highest club played would have won the trick, and East's play of another suit wouldn't affect this situation.

Suppose, in a No-Trump contract, that all players other than the one leading, is out of the led suit. For example a ♣ 2 is led, and the players in turn put down the ♠ K, ♥ A and ♦ Q. The ♣ 2 wins the trick. Only a higher club could beat the lead. Altogether, there are thirteen rounds of play, with each round, other than the first, started by the winner of the previous trick. If dummy had won a trick, then the declarer plays the next round from dummy's cards. Dummy has the lead.

After all thirteen rounds have been played, the cards are depleted. Now each side adds up their packets to see if the contract was made or set, and then the points are put on the scorecard accordingly.

Now, we might ask ourselves, just how did the partnership know what contract to bid and play for, or know just how many tricks it could win. This leads us to the discussion of how to evaluate a hand.

VI. How to Evaluate A Hand

There are several ways to evaluate a hand, but we'll deal with the standard ways in this book. Most players look at their hands in terms of a point count, giving a value not only to high cards, the **honors** (Ace, King, Queen and Jack) but to **voids** (no cards in a suit) **singletons** (one card in a suit) and **doubletons** (two in a suit).

The Point Count

This is universally followed today, having been popularized originally by Charles Goren. Each honor has a certain value.

Chart 10 Honor Values	
Ace	4 points
King	3 points
Queen	2 points
Jack	1 point

We can't look at these cards in isolation, except in No-Trump contracts, where there is no one trump suit and the high cards' values can stand by themselves. In suit contracts, having a void, a singleton or doubleton in the hand has extra value. These are called **distribution values.** The reason a void is valuable, for instance, is that the holder of a void suit can immediately trump a lead in that suit and win the trick. For example, suppose the trumps are hearts, and the bidder is void in clubs. An ace of clubs is led by the opposing partnership, and this can now be trumped by the holder of the void, negating the opponents' ace, and winning the trick easily.

Here are the standard distributional values:

Chart 11
Standard Distribution Values

Void Suit	3 points
Singleton	2 points
Doubleton	1 point

With no-trump hands, voids, singletons and doubletons can be negative, rather than positive, since there is no trump suit, and if a player is void in the led suit, he must play another suit and cannot possibly win the trick.

Opening Bid Requirements

The first one at the table to bid is known as the **opening bidder.** In the following sequence, West is the opening bidder.

North	East	South	West
Pass	Pass	Pass	One Heart

What would have happened if all four players passed?

The deal would be said to be passed, and all the cards would be thrown in, and play stopped. At least one bid must be made, other than pass, in the first four, in order for the bidding and game to continue.

In order to open the bidding, standard practice insists that a player must have at least 13 points. These 13 points, if a suit is bid, can be in honors or a combination of honors and distributional values. If the bidding is in No-Trump, they must be only in honors, and the requirements are higher, but for the time being, we'll concentrate on suit bids.

Biddable Suits

Not only must there be 13 points, but the suit bid as the strongest, the suit that will possibly be the trump suit, should have at least four, and in some instances, five cards in it. Four cards are necessary for the minor suits, Diamonds and Clubs, while five cards are the requirement for the major suits, Hearts and Spades. Of course, in advanced play, there are exceptions to this rule, but this is basic, and should be followed for now.

The four card suit should be headed by an honor, while the five card suit can be headed by a 10 in its weakest form, while an honor would be preferable. The following are examples of **biddable suits.**

♠ A 10 9 6 5
♦ J 9 5 4

In the following two hands, we can see the first with

no biddable suit, while the second has a biddable suit, spades.

Hand No. 1.

♠ 10 5 4 2   ♥ A J 5   ♦ A Q 8   ♣ Q 7 3

Although the hand contains 13 points in honors, there is really no biddable suit. There isn't a major suit of five cards headed by an honor, nor is there a minor suit of four cards headed by an honor.

Hand No. 2

♠ A J 8 5 2   ♥ 7 2   ♦ A Q 6   ♣ J 6 5

In hand no. 2 we have 12 high card or honor points plus a doubleton in hearts, which gives us 13 points. Not only that, but we have a biddable suit, the spade suit, five cards headed by two honors.

Thus, to summarize, in order to have *an opening bid of one in a suit,* it is necessary to have at least 13 points in honors and distributional value, and at least a five card major or four card minor suit.

VII. The Opening Bids

Artificial One-Club Bid

An accepted practice among some players is to open with an **artificial** One-Club bid if the hand contains two four-card major suits and at least 13 points. Suppose a player was dealt the following:

♠ A J 6 4   ♥ K J 8 5   ♦ A J   ♣ 7 6 5

We see 14 points in high cards, but no biddable suit because the majors are both four cards long. Thus, an artificial One-Club bid is made, asking the partner to bid a major suit that is his longest, if possible, so that the partnership can determine which major suit to play as trumps. The partnership will always prefer major suits to minor suits, because only four of a major bid and made is game, whereas it is necessary to bid and make five in a minor suit for game.

Responses to Opening Suit Bids of One

The purpose of bidding is to gain information so that the partnership can determine what level to bid up to, and what suit (or no-trump) to play as trumps. When an opening bidder starts at the one-level in a suit, he is telling his partner that he has a biddable suit and at least 13 points. Now it is the partner's turn to give information by his *response* to the opening bid. Here are the possible responses and the information they indicate:

1. Pass

If a partner has less than six points in high cards, he should pass. If he bids otherwise, the partnership is in trouble and won't be able to make a contract at the two-level.

2. A Raise of One over One

This is a bid in the same level as the partner's bid. For example, if the opening bid was One Diamond, a bid of One Heart or One Spade is a raise of one over one. It is not that weak a bid, but is known as a **forcing bid.** It forces the opener to make another bid, at least one.

To make this bid, a responder must have between 6 and 17 high card points, and at least a four-card suit in the suit bid. The bidding would look like this, with North opening the bidding and South responding:

North	East	South	West
1 Diamond	Pass	1 Heart	

If a responder has two four-card suits, it is always best to bid the major rather than the minor one. And if both are majors, it is best to bid the lower ranked of the two, hearts over spades

3. Two over One

In this situation, after a one bid, the partner raises it to the two-level. This can happen if the bid is a major suit, and the response is in a minor suit. A typical response would show in this situation:

North	East	South	West
1 Heart	Pass	2 Diamonds	

This bid is also forcing for at least one round, forcing the opening bidder to make another bid. In order to make this bid, a responder should have the following:

a. Five or more cards in his bid suit.

b. At least 10 points in high card points, and up to 18 points combined with distributional strength.

4. Raising Your Partner's Major Bid Suit to Two

If your partner has opened with either One Heart or One Spade, you can respond in that same suit with the following at the two-level.

a. 6 to 10 points.

b. Four cards in that major suit, or three cards headed by an honor.

The bidding would look like this:

North	East	South	West
1 Heart	Pass	2 Hearts	

5. Raising Your Partner's Major Suit Bid to Three

To bid three, you need the following:

a. 13-16 points, and four in the suit bid by the opener, headed by at least a queen.

6. Raising Your Partner's Major Bid Suit to Four

To bid at the four-level in the same major, you need

the following:

    a. Seven to 10 points in high cards.

    b. Five of that suit.

The reason the requirements are less than a raise to three is that you're ending the bidding at the four-level in a major, and going for game. At the three level, you're keeping the bidding alive, and may go even higher than a final bid of four in the major suit.

Remember, you want to get to the optimum bid level that you can make, in the right suit

7. No Trump Responses to One-Suit Bids

a. One No-Trump

This is a weak response, and you show 6-10 points and little else.

b. Two No-Trump

1. 13-15 points in high cards.

2. Strength in the other unbid suits.

3. Balanced distribution.

What you're telling your partner is that you prefer to play the hand in No-Trump, thus the requirements of balanced hands headed by honors or other strength. With this bid, you should have no more than four cards in any one suit.

c. Three No-Trump

To bid this, you need the following:

1. 16-17 points in high cards.

2. Strength in the unbid suits.

3. Balanced distribution.

8. Jump Response in a New Suit

This is a strong bid, forcing at least to game, and possibly to slam. The responder now shows the following:

a. Strong support in opener's bid suit.

b. 19 or more points, both in high cards and distributional values.

The following hand illustrates this:

♠ K 8   ♥ A K J 9 2   ♦ K Q 5 3   ♣ K 9

If your partner opened with One Diamond, you come back with a bid of Two Hearts. That's a jump response, since you could have bid One Heart, but instead purposely jumped the bidding. This is a signal to your partner that you have a very strong hand.

We now turn to Opening No-Trump Bids.

A. Opening No-Trump Bids

Instead of opening with a suit, it is possible to open with No-Trump, especially if the declarer has no solid suit to bid. Three prerequisites are necessary. They are:

1. High Card Points.
2. Balanced Distribution.
3. High Card Distribution

High Cards

16-18 points in high cards are necessary for a One No-Trump bid.

Balanced Distribution

4-3-3-3; 4-4-3-2; 5-3-3-2 are the hands necessary. We can't afford singletons or voids with No-Trump bids. In the last example, the five card suit should be a minor one; if major, we'd probably bid the major suit.

High Card Distribution

The optimum situation is a high card in at least each suit. This doesn't often happen, but at least three suits should be protected with high cards.

One No-Trump Bid

16-18 points are necessary, along with the above prerequisites.

Two No-Trump Bid

1. 21-24 high card points.
2. Balanced hand.
3. All four suits covered by honors.

Three No-Trump Bid

1. 25-27 high card points.
2. Balanced Hand.
3. All four suits covered by honors.

B. Responses to No-Trump bids

To Opening One No-Trump Bids

1. Two Clubs

This is the **Stayman Convention,** a standard convention in bridge. It shows strength in one or possibly both of the major suits, and asks the opener to rebid any four-card major suit he might have.

If the opener has both four-card major suits, he can bid either one. Then the response would be Two No-Trump, asking him to bid the other if he can.

If the opener now bids Two Diamonds to the Two Clubs response, he says in effect that he has no major suit.

2. Two Diamonds, Hearts or Spades

This bid shows a five card suit with no interest in bidding up to a game level.

3. Two No-Trumps
8-9 points and a hand fairly balanced.

4. Three No-Trump
A long minor suit of five cards or more with 7-9 points is enough to make this bid.

5. A Four Bid in a Major Suit
7-9 points and a long major suit, of at least six cards. When this bid is made, the responder is telling the opener that the bid is closed, and the hand will be played at this level in his major suit bid.

6. Four No-Trump
15-16 points with a balanced hand.

7. Six No-Trump
17-18 points with a balanced hand.

To Opening Two No-Trump Bids

1. Pass
Less than 4 points.

2. Three No-Trump
4-9 Points.

3. Three of any Suit
This is a strong forcing bid and shows the possibility of going to slam with a holding of a five card suit and at least 10 points.

4. Four in a Major Suit
8 points and a six-card suit in the major suit bid.

5. Six No-Trump
12-14 points with a balanced hand.

A. Opening Bids of Two in a Suit

This is a forcing bid, forcing the responder to answer without passing. It shows a powerful hand and a desire to get to a game contract, at least. The following is necessary to bid Two in a Suit.

1. 25 points with a good five-card suit. If there are two good five-card suits, 24 points.

2. 23 high card points with a good six-card suit.

3. 21 high card points with a good seven-card suit.

4. If a minor suit has been bid, thus requiring a five-level bid to go to game, add 2 points to A, B and C.

B. Responses to Opening Bids of Two in a Suit

When an opener starts off the bidding with two in a suit, the responder can't pass. He must bid something to keep the bidding alive.

1. Two No-Trump

Staying at the same two-level shows a very weak hand. This is considered a negative response.

2. Three in the Same Suit

7-8 points and some adequate trump support.

3. Any Other Suit Bid

The bid should be natural, showing the particular suit and its strength, and these bids are positive, not negative bids.

4. Three No-Trump

9 points, but no particular suit to bid.

Opener's Rebid

Up to this point, we've concentrated on opening bids and one response by the partner. However, in actual games, the bidding doesn't usually stop at this point, and more bids may be forthcoming. This happens if the responder's bid is positive and is in effect telling his partner, "don't stop, let's go to game or slam." Some rebids that are usual are now covered, as follows:

After a One Over One Response

In this situation, the opener has opened with a One Bid and the partner has responded at the same level. For instance:

East	South	West	North
1 Diamond	Pass	1 Spade	Pass

West's One Spade response to East's One Diamond opening bid is a One Over One bid. Remember, this is a forcing bid, rather strong. Therefore with the following strengths, the Opener's rebid would be as follows:

a. 13-15 points and a balanced hand, the rebid is One No-Trump.

To make this perfectly clear, let's now see how the bidding went.

East	South	West	North
1 Diamond	Pass	1 Spade	Pass
1 No-Trump			

At this point, go back and study the One Over One Response and what is a balanced hand. Balanced hands are discussed in the No-Trump section.

b. 12-16 points and a strong five-card suit, rebid the opening suit.

c. 12-16 points and four cards in responder's suit, rebid the responder's suit at the next level. This can also be done with three cards in responders' suit. However, if the opener has a six-card suit, he should rebid it, or go to no-trump if his hand is balanced. The following would be a rebiddable hand in the partner's suit. Let's still have the same bidding, where East has opened with One Diamond and West has responded with One Spade. Now East holds the following:

♠ K 9 6 4
♥ A 3
♦ K J 8 4 2
♣ J 5

East has 14 points, 12 in high cards and two because of his two doubletons. His five card diamond suit isn't that strong, and he has good support for responder's One Spade bid, with his four cards headed by the king. The rebid therefore should be Two Spades.

d. 19-20 points and a balanced distribution, rebid Two No-Trump.

e. 17-19 points, and a good six card suit, jump rebid in opener's suit. For example, let's follow the bidding now:

East	South	West	North
1 Diamond	Pass	1 Spade	
3 Diamonds			

The bid of Three Diamonds, skipping any two-level bid, is a jump rebid.

f. 19-20 points, jump rebid to a new suit. This is forcing to game. For example:

East	South	West	North
1 Diamond	Pass	1 Spade	Pass
3 Hearts			

By jumping the bidding into the three level, and bidding a new suit, East is telling his partner that he has 19-20 points and wants to go to game.

g. 20 points, jump right to game. This can be done by bidding Three No-Trump, or game in Opener's or Responder's suit. When jumping right to game in his own suit, the Opener should have seven trumps, but needs only four cards in responder's suit to jump to game in responder's suit.

After a Two Over One Response

Remember, this is a forcing response, but only for one round. It would look like this diagrammed:

South	West	North	East
1 Heart	Pass	2 Clubs	Pass

North's Two Clubs response is Two Over One.

a. 12-14 points, the Opener should rebid his opening suit, a weak bid.

b. 12-16 points and a balanced distribution, bid Two No-Trump.

c. 12-16 points and another biddable suit, bid the other suit.

d. 15-17 points and good trump support in partner's suit, rebid his suit at the three-level.

e. 17-19 points and a six card or longer suit, jump rebid in opener's suit.

f. 17-19 points, with good trumps, plus a singleton or void suit other than responder's suit, jump bid in responder's suit.

g. 17-19 points and a balanced distribution, go right to game with a bid of Three No-Trump.

h. 20 or more points, go right to game, or make a forcing bid to game; for example, bid a new suit at the next level.

Points Necessary to Go to Game

The important thing to remember when bidding and rebidding, is that 26 points add up to game. The 26 points are the combined points in opener's and responder's hands. Usually, the responder can know this better than the opener, and shouldn't end the bidding if there is a chance for game. For example, suppose that the responder has 13 points. He knows that the opener needed 13 points to open the bidding, and together they have at least 26 points, so he shouldn't stop the bidding short of game, but should encourage the bidding, and also, by studying the previous sections, give his partner enough information so that they wind up in the right suit or No-Trump contract.

Preemptive Bids

This type of opening bid is made where the holder of a hand containing little high card strength, but a long suit, wishes to open the bidding to force his opponent's into higher ground than they wish to be at the outset. It is generally thus used for defensive purposes, to upset the opponent's natural bids, and to force them, if possible, to bid higher levels than they wished to.

The best type of preemptive bid is in a minor suit, and the best place to make the bid is when you're sitting third in the bidding order, and there have already been two passes, first by your partner and then by one opponent. With your weak high card strength, at this point you're quite certain that the fourth player, your opponent, will come in with an opening bid or even two in a suit, a very strong bid. So now you want to get in first, and upset the applecart.

At other times, if you're the dealer and thus the first one to bid, you might want to get in a preemptive bid to upset your opponents, thus cutting their communications at the outset and forcing them into higher ground.

Here are two examples of hands that would call for an opening preemptive bid:

♠ 3 2   ♥ K 9 3   ♦ Q J 8 5 4 3 2   ♣ 3

You can now preempt with Three Diamonds. Let's assume there have been two passes to you. You know that your opponent will probably come in with a major suit bid, probably in spades. By bidding Three Diamonds, you're forcing him to come in at the three level, giving but little information to his partner. If you didn't preempt, you might be facing an opening Two Spades bid, forcing to game in all probability.

♠ Q 5   ♥ 9   ♦ K 10 3   ♣ Q 9 8 7 5 3 2

Here we can come in with a Three Club preemptive bid, again blocking the opponent's communications.

Responses to Preemptive Bids

Having recognized that his partner has opened with a preemptive bid, the responder should realize that he can't count on his partner for much in the way of card strength, but definitely on length of the suit bid.

Raise to game in a major suit. You should have at least three strong playing cards, aces or kings, in any suits. For example, if your partner preempted with Three Hearts, in this situation you go to Four Hearts.

Three No-Trump. You need stoppers in at least two of the suits not bid, with sufficient strength in the other suits.

Three of a Higher-Ranking Suit. If the preemptive bid was in a minor suit, and you have a strong major suit of your own, bid the major suit at the Three level. It is usually forcing to game.

Four of a Lower Ranking Suit, usually a minor suit. For example, the preemptive bid has been Three Hearts. You now come in at Four Clubs. This shows powerful strength, and is pushing toward a slam bid. This occurs where the opener was the dealer, and you are now first coming in with a bid.

VIII. Defensive Bidding

Up to this point, we've spoken of bidding by the opener and the responder, without any interference from the opponents. However, they often come into the bidding, either with their own strength, or defensively. Remember, bidding gives information to the partnership, and the opponents' bidding can give valuable clues to the defense of the contract.

Overcalls

An **overcall** is a bid made by the opposing partnership after an opener has started the bidding. It is made at a higher level. For example, in the following diagram, South's One Heart bid is an overcall.

North	East	South	West
Pass	1 Diamond	1 Heart	

In order to make an overcall, the bidder should have at least 13 points, and a five or six card suit. If the overcall came in at the two-level, he should have at least a six or seven card suit.

If a player has 16 or more points, and there has already been an opening bid by the opposition, he shouldn't bid an overcall, but should double. This will be discussed in a later section.

Vulnerability also comes in here. If the opponents are vulnerable, and you're not, you can overcall even with 11 or 12 points at the one-level.

Doubles

As you may remember, one of the bids that can be made by a player is a double. There are two kinds of doubles, takeout doubles and penalty doubles. The **takeout double,** which we'll discuss first, tells the partner of the doubler that he has a hand that can be opened, but he doesn't wish to announce it yet. What the takeout double forces the partner to do is bid his longest or best suit, regardless of his point count.

Takeout Doubles

Since a bidder can't announce that his double is a takeout double rather than a penalty double, the following must be done in order to construe it as a takeout double

a. It comes at the bidder's first opportunity to double.

b. It usually doubles a suit below the game level.

c. The doubler's partner hasn't bid yet.

The following diagrams show takeout doubles:

North	East	South	West
1 Heart	Double		

There is no way to misconstrue this double. All three criteria have been met. It's a takeout double.

North	East	South	West
1 Diamond	Pass	1 Heart	Double

All the criteria have been met again. East's pass is not to be construed as a bid, since, by bid, we mean an active bid in a suit or No-Trump by doubler's partner. If East had a bid already, as in the following diagram, then West's double is no longer a takeout double.

North	East	South	West
1 Heart	1 Spade	2 Diamonds	Double

Why should a player bid a takeout double rather than his own suit? Perhaps, though the doubler has opening bid strength, he doesn't really have a strong suit to bid. Or his hand is very strong, and if he merely overcalls, his partner might pass. A takeout double forces the partner to bid for one round, and thus the doubler gets valuable information about his partner's longest or best suit. If there's a fit, then the doubler and his partner can go to the correct contract in the correct suit.

Responses to Takeout Doubles

As we know, a takeout double is forcing for one round, so the partner must make some kind of bid, no matter how weak his hand is. There is one exception, however. If your partner has made the takeout double and you have 6-8 points and length in the opponent's bid suit, then if you pass, it indicates to your partner that his double is now a **penalty double.**

Let's see how this works in the following diagram.

North	East	South	West
1 Spade	Pass	2 Hearts	Double
2 Spades	Pass		

At this point you're telling your partner that you, East have 6-8 points and length in spades. So now the takeout double becomes a penalty double against the opponents making a Two Spade contract.

Let's follow another diagram, and see the correct bid after a takeout double in four instances:

North	East	South	West
1 Diamond	Double	Pass	

In this situation you are West.

a. 6-8 points and length in diamonds. You pass. East's takeout double now becomes a penalty double.

b. No more than 8 points. Bid at the lowest level, either at the one-level in Hearts or Spades, or Two Clubs, showing your weak hand.

c. 8-10 points and a **stopper** (high honor: A-K-Q) in Diamonds. Bid One No-Trump.

d. At least 13 points, enough for game. You make what is known as a **cue bid.** A cue bid is defined as a bid that is artificial, i.e. in which you don't have strength, but which cues your partner to the fact that you wish to go to game. In this instance, if you didn't have anything in Diamonds, but bid Two Diamonds (the opener's suit), it is telling your partner your bid is artificial and you wish to go to game.

Penalty Doubles

These doubles are purely to penalize the opponents for incorrectly bidding or bidding at too high a level for the strength of their cards as opposed to a takeout double which is used to get information about your partner's card strength. It is particularly valuable when the opponents are vulnerable and subject to big penalties which you garner on your side, above the line.

Doubling No-Trump

Any double of a No-Trump is considered a penalty, rather than a takeout double, even at the opening level.

Doubles of Overcalls

Remember, an overcall is a bid higher than the opener's bid by an opponent. For example, suppose you are sitting as West in this situation:

North	East	South	West
Pass	1 Heart	1 Spade	Double

Your double indicates a penalty double of South's overcall of One Spade.

By doubling, you are telling your partner:

a. You have no real support for partner's opening bid.

b. You have no strong suit of your own to bid.

c. You have some strength in opponent's bid suit, possible with middle strength, which could be defined as Q J 10 or Q 10 9 or J 10 9.

d. You have at least 12 points with a possible trick to be made in opponent's suit, or you have one definite trick with the 12 points, or you have only 10 points, but two definite tricks to be made in opponent's suit.

You shouldn't double for penalty if you have a good fit in trumps with your partner. For example, in the above situation, if you had four hearts of your own, it would be better to go for game contract on your own. By winning the game you'd make more points than through a penalty double at the one level.

IX. Bidding for Slam

The two factors necessary in bidding for a slam are strength and controls. One needs both because there can only be one trick lost when bidding Six in a suit or Six No-Trump for a small slam, and when going for a grand slam, no tricks can be lost.

By strength, we mean a high card point count, and by control we mean absolute control of the suits either by an ace or a void in the suit. With a void, you can immediately trump the lean of the opponents, and thus win the trick.

Strength

To bid for a slam, both partners must have at least 33 high card points between them. That leaves 7 high card points for the opposition. With 8 points made up of two aces held by the opponents, any bid for a small slam will probably fail. This can be overcome if the partnership bidding for slam has a void in the suit headed by one of the opponent's aces. But if there are no voids, the 33 high card points are essential.

Controls

Since the opponents lead to dummy of the first trick in each contract, and if they have the two aces or ace king in a suit they can cash in, the slam will immediately be set. Therefore it's essential that there be controls in each and every suit to prevent this. A void is a great control, as we have seen.

As the partnership continues to bid higher and higher toward that slam, often they might want to know just how many aces they have between them. To do this, an artificial bid is used through the Blackwood Convention.

Blackwood Convention

This convention, universally used, was invented by Easley Blackwood, and gives information about the number of aces in a partner's hand.

Usually the partner with the stronger hand wants to know about aces in his partner's hand. To find out this information, he artificially bids Four No-Trump, the Blackwood Convention. He is now asking for aces, and the reply he gets will tell him how many aces his partner has. Here's what the replies mean:

Chart 12
Blackwood Convention: Five Bid

No aces or four aces	Five Clubs
One ace	Five Diamonds
Two aces	Five Hearts
Three aces	Five Spades

Now, the same partner can ask for kings held, by continuing the convention and bidding Five No-Trump. The same responses will determine how many kings the partner responding has. Thus a bid of Six Spades will show three kings.

X. Declarer's Play

Once the declarer has bid for the contract, he must now play for the required tricks to make the contract. To do this, there are several strategies open to him. Some of the same tactics can be used by the defenders, as well.

Ruffing and Trumping

When a declarer is void in a suit, he can lead the suit from the hand holding cards in that suit, and trump the card in the void hand. This is called **ruffing.**

Crossruffing

Sometimes a declarer can work out a situation where he is void in one suit in his hand and another in dummy, and he continues to lean the suit and trump it, then leads the other suit and trumps it. Here's how it works. Suppose that diamonds is trump and the declarer is void in hearts in his hand, and the dummy is void in spades. The declarer leads a spade from his hand and trumps it with dummy's diamond, and then leads a heart from dummy and trumps it with is own diamond, and so on and so forth.

This is called crossruffing.

The Finesse

This is a lead to a broken sequence of high cards, usually, to take advantage of the bad position of the opponent's cards. For example, suppose we have this situation.

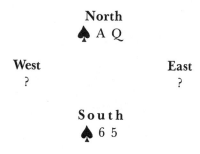

You are South, and want to take both the Ace and Queen of Spades as two tricks. You aren't sure where the King of Spades is, but from the bidding and previous play you believe it is held by West. You are on the lead. You lead the ♠ 6 to the A Q. If West has the king, he's in a bind. If he plays it, you win the trick with the Ace. If he ducks it, and plays another spade, you play the queen and it holds, then you return the ace for the other winning trick.

But of course, you can't be sure if West has the king. If he plays a ♠ 4 to your ♠ 6 lead, now you have to decide whether or not to play the queen. If the queen is played and holds the trick, you've successfully finessed it. If East holds the king, your finesse will fail.

Entries

Since the winner of the previous trick leads for the next round of play, sometimes you must make sure you have an entry into a hand so that a card can be led from it. For example, if you have high hearts in one hand, but no way to get to that hand to play them, they may become losing cards to a lead by an opponent of a different suit. Here's how this might happen. You are still South and playing out a contract at Five Clubs. A number of tricks have been played, and now West has the lead.

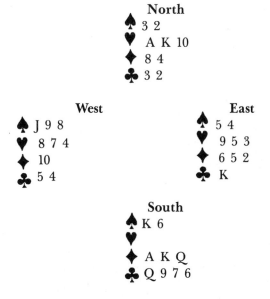

North
♠ 3 2
♥ A K 10
♦ 8 4
♣ 3 2

West
♠ J 9 8
♥ 8 7 4
♦ 10
♣ 5 4

East
♠ 5 4
♥ 9 5 3
♦ 6 5 2
♣ K

South
♠ K 6
♥
♦ A K Q
♣ Q 9 7 6

If West leads a heart, your contract plays itself. You cash in the Ace and King of Hearts, play the 10 as a winner, dumping off the ♠ 6, and you'll only lose one trick to the ♣K, which is trumps. At this point, we'll assume you've lost one trick and can only afford to lose one more.

But if the ♠J is led, you'll win it with the king, and have no way to get back to the dummy's board to cash in the hearts. You have no entry. If you had a small heart in your hand, the playing out of the hand would be no problem. That's why entries are important in bridge.

XI. **Defenders Play**

The following are general guidelines for correct defender's play. Of course, there are exceptions to every rule, and the guidelines should be taken as basic rules of play, with possible variations as you get more expert.

Leads

1. The best lead is the suit bid by your partner, since he will have an honor in it to win a trick, or it will set up a winning trick.

2. Don't lead your best suit against a suit contract, for you may give your strength too early and lose control of the play.

3. If you've seen the dummy, a good lead is always to dummy's strength, if dummy is the second to play a card.

4. If your opponents have strong trumps, conserve yours. But if they have weak trumps and intend to make their tricks by ruffing and crossruffing, play trumps and deplete them of this opportunity by removing their trumps.

5. If you have a singleton, play it, so that your partner can return the same suit for you to trump.

6. When playing against a No-Trump contract, the usual lead is the fourth highest card of your longest and strongest suit.

Other Defensive Plays

1. Second Hand Low

As a general rule, second hand plays low. Thus, if a high card is led to you, and you are second, play your lowest card.

2. Third Hand High

If you are the third hand, play high. It will either win the trick or force out an even higher card from the fourth hand, and allow you control if you have another high card in that suit.

3. Cover an Honor with an Honor

Honors are the high cards; aces, kings, queens and jacks. If a queen is led to you, and you are third to play, cover it with a king. You'll either win the trick or force out the ace, so with one card, the king, you've forced out two high cards of the opponents.

XII. A Final Word

We've covered the basics of rubber contract bridge. There are other forms, such as duplicate, which should be played only after you've mastered the basics first.

Remember, contract bridge is a partnership game. Two people form a partnership. Mistakes are frequently made, even by the best of players.

Keep your temper and be a good partner. Study this book and practice and you'll find yourself enjoying one of the great games of the world. And good luck!

NEW - CHESSCITY MAGAZINE
Free Online Chess Magazine

Subscribe to our free online chess magazine with articles, columns, gossip, and more. *Chess is our Game!*

Chess City is a sprawling metropolis of chess information, a magazine with the latest news and analysis, to gossip, trivia, and fun features. Travel around the world to visit the most fascinating chess competitions, preview books long before they hit the shelves, and read informative columns on openings, middlegames, endings, tactics, strategies, mates, and much more.

Chess City is the most exciting new chess web site on the World Wide Web. You'll be able to catch up on the latest news and find out where the tournaments are, get secret tips from top professionals and trainers, read about the exploits of the Whiz Kids, and delve into the history and personalities of the chess world. View games online with commentary by Cardoza authors, or download chess games annotated with words, not hieroglyphics.

Go to www.chesscity.com for details

FREE MAGAZINE!

I think you'll love my magazine, Avery Cardoza's PLAYER, and will want to subscribe. So I'm offering you a free copy. PLAYER is a glossy magazine with beautiful photography and great editorial on the gambling lifestyle; your favorite games, the latest gadgets and toys, celebrities, insider looks at casinos, and money-making strategies on hold'em, blackjack, and more. Give us a try—on me!

Avery Cardoza

SEND THIS CARD IN NOW AND I'LL EVEN PAY THE POSTAGE!

☐ **YES!** Send me my free copy (with no obligation)

☐ **YES!** Send me my free copy plus I subscribe for 6 issues at $19.95
(33% off the newsstand price—7 issues total)

☐ **YES!** Send me my free copy plus I subscribe for 12 issues at $29.95
(50% off the newsstand price—13 issues total)

Name _____
(please print)

Address _____ Apt. _____

City _____ State _____ Zip _____

E-mail (Receive a FREE subscription to Avery Cardoza's e-mail gambling newsletters. You also receive free bonuses, discounts, and more!)